# Where to Start

There's many different reasons why you might be thinking of selling your property, and the process that lies ahead may feel overwhelming. The good news is that you're not on your own. This Complete Guide to Selling Your Property will walk you through the various steps, answer your questions, and give you some pointers for getting the most out of your sale.

We will also let you know what to look out for when choosing an experienced Real Estate Agent to be your trusted ally and advocate. At Calibre Real Estate, we know this process inside out. We have a reputation for honesty, transparency and an unmatched personal service, and we're here to help you make your next move smooth, fast and stress-free.

# Steps to selling property

┌─ THINKING OF SELLING YOUR HOME? ─┐

The process of selling can feel confusing or overwhelming,
but an informed, proactive and strategic approach is the best way to set
yourself on course for a successful outcome.

## 01 Where to Start

It's important to understand the current state of the market in your area, and what buyers are looking for, so that you can decide when to sell and begin to take steps to make your property stand out from the crowd. You will also need to choose how to sell your house, and find yourself an agent you can trust to support you throughout the process of selling.

page 03

## 02 Property Appraisal

Get a free and comprehensive property appraisal to find out how much your house is currently worth, and how it compares to other properties on the market in the area. This can also include recommendations for small improvements you could make to boost your chances of a fast sale at a good price.

page 66

## 03 Choosing How to Sell

The most common methods of selling real estate are auction or private property sales. Each approach has its own benefits, challenges and risks, so it's important to understand your options and make an informed choice about how to sell.

page 11

## 04 Pricing Your Home

Setting an appropriate asking price is crucial for attracting buyers, selling fast, and getting the most out of your property sale. Find out more about the dangers of overpricing, and what your agent can do to help you get it right for the market in your area.

page 17

YOUR WAY HOME

## 05 Marketing Your Property

The next step is getting your property seen by the right people, and making it stand out from the crowd. From high quality print brochures and signage to strategic social media and search engine marketing, it is important to know how to market your property in a way that's strategic, targeted and highly effective.

page 46

## 06 Showing Your Home

Showcasing your home to its full potential is the best way to encourage more, and higher, offers from motivated buyers. Your checklist when selling your home should include thorough cleaning, minor repairs, and home styling, as well as paying attention to your outside areas and curb appeal.

page 20

## 07 Negotiating

Negotiating the final purchase price is an essential part of the process when selling a house, but it can feel awkward and stressful. With an experienced agent who has successfully completed many recent property sales in your area, you need to be able to trust their advice to get the best outcome.

page 24

## 08 Completing the Sale

It can take anything from 30 to 90 days to take care of the legal processes and paperwork, and reach a completion date. This includes the exchange of contracts, a cooling off period, and any other conditions that need to be fulfilled. Your solicitor should keep you updated throughout this final stage of the house selling process so that you can make arrangements and get moving!

page 26

At Calibre Real Estate, we have the local knowledge and marketing expertise to get your house noticed by the right buyers and sold at the best price. Our property sales history in your area reflects the proven success of our approach, on behalf of our valued customers. Throughout the process, you have an expert on hand to support and advise you, and we are committed to getting the best results for our customers. That's why so many customers recommend us to friends and family!

## To buy or sell first?

When it comes to moving house, one of the most common questions people have is whether it's best to buy first or sell first – or simultaneously. There is no simple answer to this as it will depend on your own financial situation and stage of life, as well as the current market conditions.
It's important to consider the different scenarios and what they would mean for you when selling your home.

# Buying first

## The benefits:

Less time pressure as you house hunt, so you can take the time to find your ideal next home and avoid over-paying.

You can move straight into your new home when you're ready, rather than potentially having to find a stop-gap and paying rent for a period of time.

Opportunity to renovate before you move in.

Gives you flexibility when it comes to agreeing on a settlement date with the seller as you don't need to move in right away.

## The risks:

It's difficult to budget accurately when you don't know what your house is actually going to sell for.

You could end up paying off the loans on two properties while you're waiting to sell your own home.

Pressure to sell might mean that you end up accepting a lower offer, especially if supply outweighs demand (a buyer's market).

If the market slows down, it could take longer than expected to sell, and this could cause problems if you're relying on bridging finance.

CALIBRE
REAL ESTATE

# Selling first

## The benefits:

You know exactly what your budget is and how much wiggle room there is.

You have the option to use the sale proceeds to buy your new home.

No time pressure to accept an offer if it's lower than you were expecting.

No risk of being burdened with two mortgages that overlap.

If you sell at a good time, and then prices fall, you could get more for your money on your next property.

## The risks:

If your home sells quickly, you may be under pressure to find a new property, and this can lead to over-paying or over-compromising.

If you have to rent somewhere in the interim, this adds to your cost and effectively means moving twice.

If property prices go up after you sell, you may end up getting less for your money on your next purchase.

At Calibre, we can help you to assess your individual circumstances, understand the current market conditions, and advice you regarding which steps to take towards successfully selling your house.
Talk to an expert today.

# Prepare emotionally

At Calibre Real Estate, we're here to help your house selling process go smoothly, and to support you from start to finish so that it doesn't have to be a stressful experience. However, the process of selling your home requires effort and energy, and is likely to bring up a mixture of emotions.

It's all very well following the practical steps on your house selling checklist, but if you don't take the time to prepare emotionally up front, you risk having second thoughts further down the line or being de-railed by the emotional upheaval at the least convenient moment.

Before you crack on, remind yourself of your reasons and motivations for selling, and take stock of your emotions. Only then can you begin to work through the stages of selling your home, and stay on track, without the stress.

# Know your local market

One of the very first steps of selling property, and getting the best price when selling your home, is to understand your local market. Some basic online research, using popular real estate sites such as www.realestate.com.au and www.domain.com.au will give you a good idea of the kinds of properties for sale in your area, and a realistic sense of the value of your home to potential buyers.

This is just a starting point as the market is always fluctuating, and property prices can differ for multiple reasons. For a more in-depth and reliable insight into the current demand in your area, and a reasonable asking price for a property like yours, you should arrange a market appraisal from a trusted local agent.

At Calibre Real Estate, we have a proven track record of selling properties like yours and pride ourselves on our thorough, up to date understanding of the local market. One of our experts would be happy to visit your home and give you a full and detailed appraisal, with no obligation.

# Choose when to sell

> Across Australia, the most popular time for selling property is Spring because of the warm and pleasant weather. Brisbane, though, has the advantage of great weather throughout the year so you don't need to feel restricted to Spring when selling your home.

## Spring

Spring tends to encourage buyers to visit open homes, and often shows properties in their best light. This helps to generate interest and competition. But with many other sellers also opting for Spring, buyers have plenty of choice and you might have to work harder to make your property stand out from the crowd.

## Summer

Summer can see a lull in property sales as many people go on holiday or take time off with friends and family over the festive season. On the other hand, if you can get your house on the market in the run-up to Christmas you could benefit from those motivated buyers who want to move and settle before the holidays kick in. With fewer properties on the market, you might get more interest and a higher sale price.

## Autumn

Autumn is often a very busy time for the property market. Many buyers and sellers want to move before the end of the financial year, and the uninterrupted 12 weeks of Autumn is an appealing time to get it done. As the market thrives, though, this also means fierce competition.

## Winter

Winter typically slows things down as the weather puts people off – buyers and sellers alike. But the milder climate of Brisbane gives you the opportunity to take advantage of the lull and get your property noticed, with less competition.

Of course, you also need to think about your own diary and work around any particular dates, occasions or holidays that might interfere with your house sale.

It's important to find a time that works for you and your family.

# Different Ways to Sell a Property

There is more than one way to sell a property, and it all comes down to your specific circumstances and priorities. In the end, the best way to sell your house is the method that suits you and your local market.

The most common methods of sale are auction or private sale. Each approach has its own rules, protocols, benefits and challenges, so make sure you understand the options and can make an informed decision about what's best for you.

Your Calibre Real Estate agent will be able to give you a run-down of the pros and cons of the different ways to sell property, as well as advice on selling a house like yours in your particular area. We know the local market, and the approaches that have worked well for recent property sales, and can support you to get a fast sale at the highest price.

## Auction

A **real estate auction** takes place on a single date, when prospective buyers can publicly bid on the property. The seller can set a reserve price at the lower limit of what they are prepared to accept. Assuming bidding reaches or exceeds the reserve price, the property will go to the highest bidder.

Selling property at auction can be a fast and efficient way of getting a good price as it creates an environment of competition. This also makes it very intense, with a focused marketing campaign in the lead up to the day itself.

If you decide to auction your house, you can still accept an offer before the day of the auction, or decide not to sell on the day but continue negotiations with the interested buyers. So, either way, it can pay off. Once a bidder has "won" the auction, contracts will be signed on the day, the deposit will be paid, and the buyer can't unexpectedly pull out.

### Challenges:

High stress day so it's important to have a good advisor on hand.

### The benefits:

An auction creates a sense of urgency and competition so will often achieve a better price.

A private auction secures an unconditional contract and a set settlement date, there and then.

Auctions can attract more prospective buyers because there isn't a set asking price.

Selling a house at auction comes with the protection of a set reserve price, and terms of sale, so you don't risk selling at a lower price than this pre-agreed level.

If you auction your house, there is no upper limit on the sale price, so you may get much more than you expected.

# Private Treaty / Sale

A private treaty / private sale involves a property listing and an asking price. Prospective buyers generally get in touch with the agent to arrange viewings and make their offers, and the agent presents these to the seller for consideration.

In a real estate private sale, an offer doesn't constitute a binding contract – there is still room for negotiation and the option for either party to pull out. An experienced agent will be able to negotiate with potential buyers on the seller's behalf, to try and secure the best price.

You might choose to put your house up for sale by private treaty if you're not in a rush to get moving and are happy to wait for the right offer. Private house sales tend to give the seller more control, and the opportunity to compare and negotiate on different offers before making a decision.

## Challenges:

Less urgency and competition means the whole process can take longer.

Buyers could pull out of the contract during their finance, building and pest, or other special conditions.

Buyers could change their mind during the cooling-off period.

## The benefits:

Private house sales give the seller more control over the process.

Private house sales give you more time to compare offers.

A private treaty is generally less intense than an auction, and can therefore feel less stressful.

Houses sold by private treaty give both parties the flexibility of a longer settlement period.

Private house sales allow for the asking price to be adjusted over time, to reflect the interest from prospective buyers and fluctuations in the market.

A fixed asking price is simpler for buyers.

# Don't wait to declutter

Sorting, clearing, and decluttering may not be the most glamorous stage of the process when selling a house, but it can have a surprising impact on the look and feel of your home when it comes to marketing. A minimal look, with fewer personal items on display, can make the rooms feel bigger, brighter and cleaner, and makes it easier for buyers to picture themselves living in the house.

The sooner you begin to clear unnecessary clutter and re-organise shelves and surfaces, the sooner you can begin to show off your house at its best – both in marketing photography and when potential buyers come to visit.

This also helps to reduce the work and stress of actually packing up and moving once your house has sold – win, win!

WAY HOME YOUR

# How to choose the best way to sell your house

This is where an experienced and knowledgeable real estate agent is invaluable. They can give you personalized home selling advice, based on your own specific circumstances, and guide you towards the best way to sell your type of property in your area.

## This specialist real estate sales advice will take into account the following factors:

- ☑ Type and location of your property
- ☑ Local market conditions and trends
- ☑ Your priorities and preferences – sell quickly, save on costs, minimize risk, stay in control, get the best price...

The more that your agent understands about your motivations and priorities for selling your property, the more they will be able to help you to secure the best outcome.

For over 13 years, Calibre Real Estate has led the way in putting our customers first, understanding their needs and preferences, and delivering outstanding results with every sale. We're working on your behalf to get you the best out of your property sale experience, and our track record speaks for itself.

# Find a great agent

A great real estate agent acts as your expert advisor and personal guide when selling your home. They should have in-depth market insights, extensive marketing experience, and a recent track record of successful property sales in your local area. This is where we excel.

At Calibre Real Estate, we have specialist knowledge of Brisbane's North West, an unparalleled record of recent sales in the area, and a commitment to getting the best outcomes for our customers.

Contact the team on 07 3367 3411 and let's start your house selling journey.

# Pricing Your Home

When setting an asking price it's always tempting to go high, but in reality your house is only worth what a buyer is willing to pay for it. If you aim too high, you can end up putting off the right buyers and attracting the wrong ones, which makes for a long, drawn out and frustrating sale process. On the other hand, pricing too low might attract lots of buyers but can mean you lose out on your potential property value.

## The right property pricing should:

- Attract the right kinds of buyers
- Give you the best chance of achieving a good sale price
- Help you to sell quickly and easily

Knowing how to price your home for a fast and successful sale comes down to an understanding of the local real estate market, and recent property sales in your area, as well as an awareness of anything that might make your property stand out from the crowd – for better or worse. A free real estate property value estimate is a good place to start.

## The importance of getting it right:

- Attract the right buyers
- Encourage higher offers
- Achieve a faster and smoother sale

- Generate more interest
- Avoid having to reduce the asking price later

## Possible reasons behind overpricing

- Seller overpaid for the property originally
- Allowing for bargaining and negotiation
- Moving to a pricier area
- Unrealistic house valuation
- Emotional attachment to the home

- Over-investment in renovations
- Financial need
- Lack of market research
- Gut feeling, or opinion of family and friends

## Dangers of overpricing

- The asking price is the main factor that will get your house noticed by interested buyers in the first place – don't let them write it off before they've even seen it.

- If your property price estimate is too high, your buyer may struggle to secure their loan as the lender's realistic house valuation won't stack up. This can mean the sale is delayed or falls through completely.

- If your house sits on the market for a long time with no sale, buyers will become wary.

- Buyers are always comparing multiple similar properties as they hunt for the right one, and perception of your house being overpriced can result in negative reactions.

- Reducing the price later makes your property seem less desirable. Many prospective buyers will have already come and gone, and you will have lost that initial buzz of interest and activity.

- Costs can stack up as you wait to sell, with extra mortgage payments, taxes and maintenance work.

- The wrong price will attract the wrong buyers, so viewings won't translate into offers.

# How your Real Estate agent can help?

- A free property appraisal to give you a realistic house value estimate.

- Marketing savvy, strategy and incentives to help you achieve the highest realistic sale price.

- Market research and analysis to give you a clear picture of comparative property prices in your area, and recent sales of similar properties.

- Up to date insights into market activity and trends.

- Advice about the things you can do to help boost your property value, such as home improvements and repairs.

- An estimate of your net proceeds, after fees and taxes.

- Expert negotiation on your behalf.

It's important to remember that no agent can control your property value or guarantee you a certain sale price. The role of your agent is to plan an effective marketing and exposure strategy, guided by concrete market analysis and recent sales, that capitalizes on the potential of your property.
Choose an agent based on their knowledge and experience, not on false promises.

# Adding Value, House Styling & Showing Your Home

## Showing your home

An open house inspection is an excellent opportunity to present your house at its best to as many buyers as possible. Open homes usually last around an hour, and the great thing about drawing all of the interested buyers through the door within this short window of time is that it generates a buzz of interest and a sense of competition.

Opening your home to all interested buyers on a set day also means you can put all of your energy into preparing your property – inside and out – and showcasing it at its very best. The idea is to make it as easy as possible for potential buyers to be able to picture themselves living there.

If you really want to make your open home inspection count, never under-estimate the importance of preparation. Try to look at your home through the eyes of a potential buyer and think about what you can do to present it at its best. It might sound like a lot of hard work, but a few small changes can go a long way. When presenting a house for sale, you can actually add value to your home with some minor home improvements and subtle house styling.

Professional house styling is an excellent way of showcasing your property in the best possible light, and strategic home staging can help to intentionally highlight its major selling points. This might involve re-arranging your current furniture or hiring furniture from a professional property stylist who knows how to make buyers fall in love the moment they walk through the door! If you want to drive more offers, and maximum profit from your sale, ask your agent about home improvements that add value and home staging that will wow your buyers. Here are some of our tips on the little things you can do before your open house inspection to add value to your home – with or without an interior stylist.

## Lights

- During the showing, open all blinds and curtains to let in plenty of natural light so that your rooms feel bright, airy and spacious.
- Use lighting to create a cosy and homely atmosphere, and to highlight the best aspects of each room.
- Avoid overhead lighting that can make rooms look stark and characterless.
- The careful arrangement of lamps can help smaller rooms feel bigger, and large rooms feel more cosy and intimate.
- Use lighting to draw the eye towards the prime "living areas", like a breakfast or dining area, chairs by a fireplace, or a cosy snug.

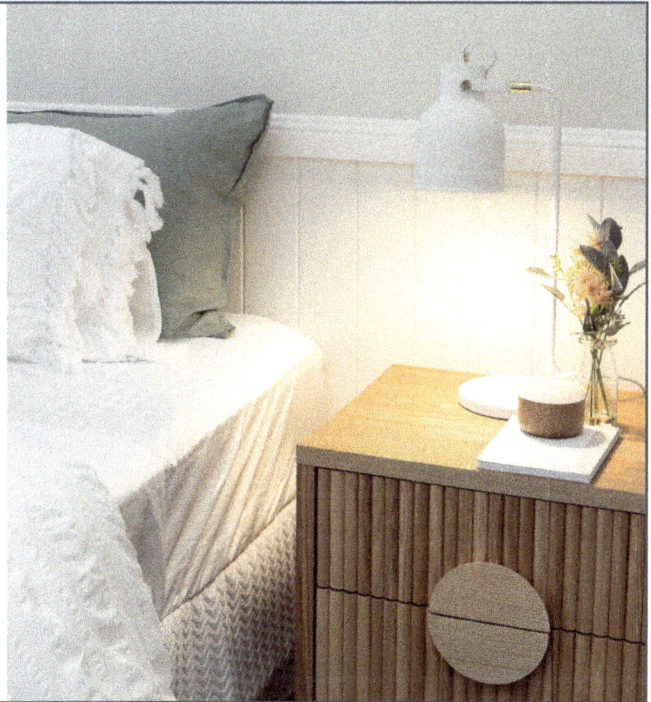

## Kitchen

- Make sure the kitchen is as clean and tidy as it can be.
- Clear kitchen surfaces of any clutter or unnecessary items.
- Remove personal photos, messages, reminders or artwork from the refrigerator to help buyers begin to picture the kitchen as their own.

## Bathrooms

- Thoroughly clean and tidy the bathrooms.
- Remove clutter from surfaces, sink areas, around the bathtub, and in the shower, keeping only the essentials.
- Remove kids' bath toys or store neatly.
- Hang clean, dry towels in just one or two colours.
- Check caulking around bathtubs and showers, and repair if necessary.
- Use candles or air fresheners to make the room smell fresh.

## 🛋 Living areas

- Clear surfaces and remove clutter.

- Rearrange or remove some furniture to make rooms feel as big and spacious as possible.

- Refresh the paint in any rooms that look tired or scuffed.

- Replace faded or peeling wallpaper.

- Steam clean carpets and curtains if necessary.

- Clean your windows, inside and out.

- Repair worn or damaged woodwork, such as skirting.

- Work your way through a checklist of minor repairs, such as doors and windows that stick or creak, loose door knobs, and broken light switches.

- Remove unnecessary clutter from your attic, basement and closets (you may want to consider a garage sale, or putting some items into storage while presenting your home for sale).

## 🏠 Exterior / Outside

- Look at your house from a buyer's perspective and think about first impressions.

- Make sure your front entrance looks clean, neat and welcoming.

- Paint or replace your front door if it looks tired, dated or worn.

- Re-touch the paint on external trim, shutters, and any other exterior features that are in need of a refresh.

- Clear gutters and check for dry rot.

- Check the condition of the roof and make small repairs, such as replacing loose tiles.

- Keep "curb appeal" in your mind at all times!

## Backyard / Garden

- Pull up weeds, lay some fresh mulch and consider adding a few attractive plants.

- Trim vegetation around windows, doors and decking to give a neat impression and show off architectural details.

- Clear patios or decking of things like barbecues, garden games and toys.

- Move garbage cans into the garage, as well as old building materials and any other clutter, so that the perimeter of the house is clear and tidy.

- Prune overgrown bushes and trees.

- Keep the lawn freshly cut and fertilized.

# Negotiating the Property Sale

A private sale/treaty will typically involve some amount of back and forth between you and your prospective buyer(s) before you agree on a selling price that suits both parties. Negotiation when selling a house is all part of the normal process, but it can feel uncomfortable and stressful. This is where it's vital that you have confidence in your agent and can lean on their experience and negotiating skill. They will know how to negotiate effectively on your behalf, using tried and tested negotiation strategies to get the best outcome for you.

## A few points to keep in mind:

- ☑ Negotiating the house price is a very common part of the buying and selling process, so don't be afraid of it!
- ☑ If buyers are serious, they will either make their best and final offer up front, or be prepared to negotiate.
- ☑ Know when to walk away – if a buyer is insistent on offering well below the listing price or is making it very difficult to proceed, it's important not to feel pressured into accepting a lower offer. Again, your agent should be able to advise you on when it's best to break off negotiations.

## HERE ARE SOME TIPS ON HOW TO NEGOTIATE

Start with a fair and appropriate asking price, based on market research of recent similar property sales in your local area. This is your first step towards attracting buyers who will be willing to make reasonable offers and negotiate to secure the sale.

You should also take stock of your personal position and circumstances as this will inform your negotiation tactics. Do you need to sell fast or can you afford to wait for the right buyer and the right offer? Is there lots of interest and competition from buyers? These factors affect the strength of your position when negotiating your house price.

Equally, consider your buyer's position and motivations. If they are competing with lots of others for your property, or are keen to move quickly, they will likely be willing to pay more in order to secure a fast settlement. Know the strength of your hand, but also be open to compromise in order to achieve an outcome that suits both parties.

Be aware that you most likely have some emotional attachment to your home which can influence your negotiation strategies and approach. On the other hand, real estate agent negotiation tactics are more objective and detached from your personal feelings as the homeowner. It's important that you trust your agent and can be led by them so that you can make an informed decision and get the best results from your property negotiation.

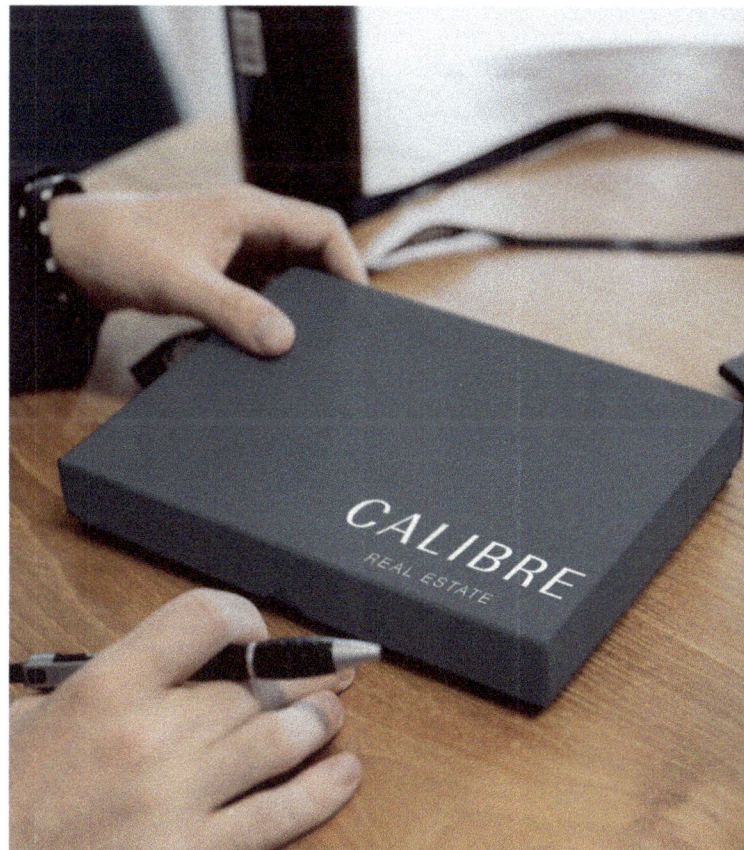

At Calibre, we are committed to getting the best outcomes for our clients. We put ourselves in your shoes and work on your behalf, with honest and transparent communication along the way. We can give you expert advice about how to negotiate selling a house, and guide you to a successful outcome with our proven negotiation strategies. Get in touch today to find out more about our negotiating experience and results in your area.

# Completing the Property Sale

## What Happens Next

Once you've agreed on the contract and all parties have signed, your agent will send a copy to both solicitors to proceed with the legal component of the sales process. The exact steps can vary, but this generally involves a cooling off period, finance, building & pest, any other conditions, and then settlement.

### 1. Signing the Contract

The actual exchange of contracts might happen after a short period of negotiation. Once the sale price is agreed, the contracts can be drawn up and the buyer will pay a deposit (up to 10% of the sale price). If you sell your property at auction, the exchange of contracts will happen on the day, with no cooling-off period nor any other conditions.

### 2. Cooling-Off

Private sales can include a 5 day cooling off period. This allows the buyer to terminate the contract with the seller without penalty.

### 3. Conditions

The most common conditions that buyers opt for are a finance clause, and a building and pest inspection, but there may be others, all subject to your approval, agreed upon in writing, and generated by a solicitor.

### 4. Settlement

The property settlement can take anything from 30 to 90 days, but your solicitor should cover off all of the necessary paperwork and keep you updated on how it's progressing. You can use this time to carry out any repairs that you agreed with the buyer during negotiations, and were flagged in the building and pest report. You should also make sure that your finances are in order (get your mortgage discharge signed off), and prepare for your move.

### 5. Move

Arrange movers for your agreed completion day (a local recommendation is usually a good way to go!). Make sure not to leave anything in your property that you haven't agreed with the buyers, and leave all house, garage, shed and letterbox keys for the new owners.

# The Contract of Sale

The contract of sale sets out the specifics of the sale, including details of the property, conditions of sale, agreed sale price, dates for exchange of contract and settlement, and more. It details the particulars of your property sale, and stands alongside the standard legal terms and conditions of any real estate transaction.

This is a crucial document so it's important that you read and understand it in full. If you have any questions about your contract of sale, your real estate agent should be able to give further explanation and clarity.

The exact process for signing and exchanging contracts can differ from state to state. In Queensland, your agent is responsible for preparing the contract of sale and accepting the buyer's deposit on your behalf once both parties have signed.

# Bank Valuation

Depending on your agreed upon conditions, the buyers of your property may wish to have a building and pest inspection completed prior to settlement to check for any structural or pest (generally termite) related issues. This is an opportunity for buyers to gain peace of mind and clarify any issues they may have noticed upon their visual inspection. The inspections are carried out by licensed professionals and are at the buyers' expense.

# Conveyancing - Settlements

Conveyancing is the process of transferring the ownership of a property from the seller to the buyer. It is a complex process, with no room for error, as it must be carried out according to property settlement law. This is why we recommend enlisting the services of a conveyancer or solicitor. They can give you a better idea of the role and responsibilities of a conveyancer, and what to expect on settlement day itself. We will also give you some tips about what to look for and what to ask when choosing a conveyancer or solicitor for your property sale.

# Preparing for Settlement

The property settlement date is the date on which the buyer pays the balance of the agreed purchase price. According to property settlement law, this is when the title of the property is transferred from the seller to the buyer. Here's a brief run down of how settlement works:

- The house sale settlement can only take place once the contract has been signed by both seller and buyer, the cooling off period is over, and any special conditions have been met.

- They will then communicate with the buyer's conveyancer or solicitor to agree on a settlement date.

- Your conveyancer or solicitor will prepare the documents for transferring the title of the property to the new owner, as well as settlement statements, including details of things like updated council rates.

- On the day, both solicitors and/or conveyancers (and lenders if necessary) will meet to exchange funds for the signed mortgage documents and the title to the house. At this point, the house movers can kick into gear!

# What Are the Costs Associated with Selling a Property?

Whatever your reasons and motivations for selling your house, it can be an emotional and challenging time. One of the ways to reduce stress and headaches is to be fully informed about what to expect, and how much you need to budget for the process itself. The cost of selling a house adds up to more than just the amount you spend on your new property, but if you start out with a good idea of the fees associated with selling a house, you can plan and budget appropriately.

## Advertising and Marketing

One of the most important roles of your real estate agent is to advertise and market your property to generate maximum interest. A range of digital marketing channels and print media will be combined to form a strategic marketing campaign. Most agencies will charge marketing costs on top of the agent's commission in order to cover these various services.

### Digital marketing includes:

- Digital brochures
- Real estate portal listings
- Social media
- Professional photography
- Drone footage

### Print marketing includes:

- Signage
- Property brochures
- Newspaper and magazine advertisements
- Professional copywriting

Your agent will use their experience and local market insights to develop a tailored marketing campaign for your property, in your area. This is a specialist service that can make a huge difference to the speed and efficiency of your sale, and to the all-important sale price itself. For this reason, advertising and marketing can add anything from several hundred to several thousand dollars to the cost of selling a house. With the right agent, this investment will pay off.

# Real Estate Agent's Commission

The agent's commission forms a key portion of the cost of selling a house. You are paying for specialist expertise, industry experience, local market knowledge, and access to valuable contacts, techniques and technologies that will help you to sell your house quickly, and at the best price.
Your agent will also be your advisor and advocate throughout the process, answering your questions, providing support, and negotiating on your behalf.

There is no standard commission rate in Queensland so you will find that the rates and methods vary between agencies. An agent may charge a flat fee, a percentage of the sale price, or a tiered commission, so it's important that you discuss this in advance and agree on a rate and structure before signing a contract.

When you find the right agent and are ready to get started, you must both complete an Appointment To Act form. This is a service agreement that sets out the rights and obligations of both parties – you and your agent. Their commission, fees and expenses should be clearly laid out in this form, and you should make sure that you understand how much you are likely to pay, and when. Once you have discussed and agreed on terms, you will both need to sign the agreement. The commission is usually payable on the settlement of the sale.

# Bank Valuation

The buyers' financier may want to get their own valuation in order to secure their finance approval for the purchase. This is commonly a part of a finance clause on a contract of sale. The buyers' financier will want to get their own valuation in order to secure their finance approval for the purchase.

# Pest and Building Inspection Reports

A detailed inspection compares your home with other similar properties and highlights any issues with the construction, workmanship and condition of the property. The report will identify any areas of deterioration or poor maintenance, as well as potential hazards. It pays to commission an in-depth report before you sell because it will either strengthen your negotiating position or prepare you to adjust your expectations.

## Solicitor & Legal Fees

The cost of selling a house will inevitably include some associated legal fees. These relate to your conveyancer or solicitor for their service in legally transferring the ownership of the property to the buyer. After you accept an offer from a buyer, your solicitor or conveyancer will manage the contracts and legal processes that follow.

It is not a legal requirement to work with a conveyancer or solicitor, but it is the best way of ensuring that all of the legal boxes are ticked and nothing falls through the cracks. The process of selling a property is complex and you can't afford to make mistakes. A licensed conveyancer or solicitor will charge their own rates for this work, and these can vary from agency to agency.

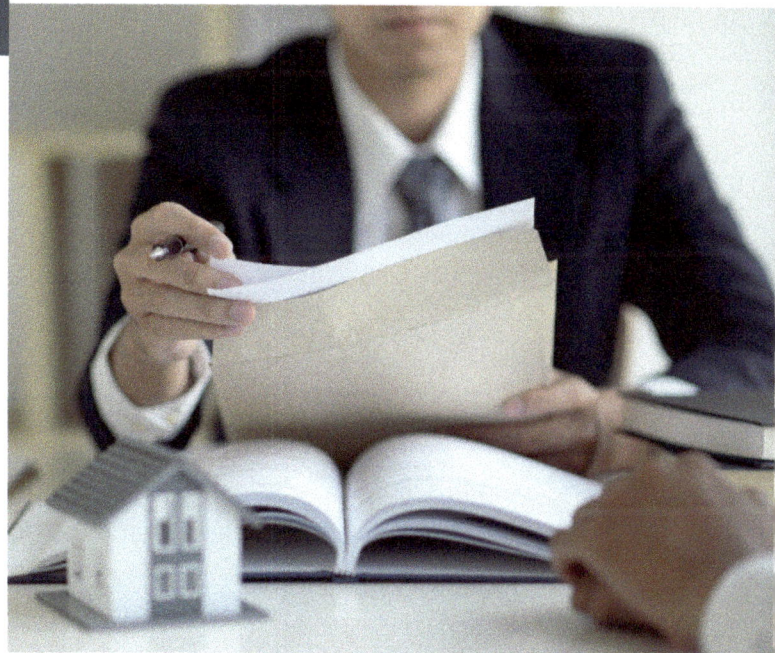

# Financial Fees

When such large sums of money are involved, it's a good idea to find a financial advisor who specialises in home loan finance. They can help you get your finances in order for your sale, and a potential new purchase, and support you to make smart decisions.

# Maintenance Costs & Styling

Preparing your property for sale, and getting it in the best condition to attract buyers, is likely to involve some financial outlay. This might sound counter-intuitive, but a little money spent on maintenance and home styling can translate into a premium sale price down the line – don't lose sight of that!

You should carry out any necessary maintenance and repairs that might put off potential buyers, such as leaks and water damage, peeling wallpaper, and scuffed or damaged woodwork. A fresh coat of paint on tired or marked walls can work wonders to make your home feel clean, bright and fresh. It's also important to pay attention the outside areas, tidying up the garden and creating a welcoming entrance.

Depending on the condition of your property, you may be able to do all of the work yourself or you may need to pay contractors and professional cleaners along the way. Your real estate agent will be able to advise you about which works are essential and will have maximum impact on your sale, and which can be left for the future owners.

Styling your home for marketing materials and buyer inspections plays a powerful role in generating interest and offers, and driving up the sale price. You can make small changes to de-clutter, de-personalise and re-arrange the setup of the rooms even while still living in the home, but if you're moving out before selling you can make an even bigger impact with a furniture package setup. We offer Calibre Interior Design services, where we work with you to style and present your home at its best, using Calibre's furniture styling packages.

# Moving Fees

When considering the cost of selling a house, it's easy to forget about moving fees. It's unlikely that you will have the time and resources to personally move all of your furniture and possessions from your old property to your new home, so it's important to factor in the cost of a removals company. These can be charged at a fixed or an hourly rate, so make sure you know what the agreement is up front.

## Miscellaneous Expenses

The average cost of selling a property can include a range of additional miscellaneous expenses. These are costs that will apply to certain house sales, but not all.

### Capital Gains Tax

If you are selling a rental property, holiday house or vacant land, you should factor Capital Gains Tax into your costs. This is because you are selling a second home or plot of land that counts as an asset, so you are required to pay tax on the profits from the sale.

### Strata and/or Council Fees

When you sell your property, there may be some outstanding council rates and strata fees to pay. These are recurring fees that are usually paid every quarter, so you need to check whether there is anything further to pay before the property actually changes hands.

At Calibre Real Estate, we understand that you want to keep the cost of selling your house to a minimum, while also doing everything you can to secure the best price in good time. We can help you find this balance. The associated costs and fees might send your head spinning, but the experts at Calibre are on hand to break it all down for you.

Our friendly and dedicated team is ready and waiting to take the stress out of your move. We can help you to understand what you're getting for your money at every stage, to spend the money where it counts, and to achieve a sale price that makes it all worth it.

Whether you are ready to sell or just want some more information about the process, we are happy to help. Contact us today for a free property appraisal.

# Real Estate Agent Commission

## Understanding Agent Commission

When you choose an agent to support you with your property sale, you are trusting them with one of the biggest and most important transactions there is – both emotionally and financially. You want to be confident that they have the experience and expertise to get the job done, and that they are going to work hard on your behalf to secure the best possible results.

Real estate agent commission on selling a house can vary dramatically, so you need to know what you're getting for your money. It's crucial that you don't just choose the agent with the lowest real estate commission fee, without doing your research – you could end up paying a high price for this in the long run.

## What is an Agent's Commission?

The real estate sales commission for selling property is the service fee that the agent earns from the sale price. This is agreed up front and is the agent's fee for their services in helping you sell your home. There may be additional fees to pay for particular marketing and advertising services, on top of the agent's commission rate, and again these should be clearly stated up front.

The bottom line is that you should make sure that you understand exactly what your real estate agent's commission fee includes, and what you will be expected to pay on top of that, before you sign an agreement and enlist their services to sell your home. That way, you can budget accordingly and won't get any nasty surprises. A good and trustworthy agent will always be happy to discuss the details of their commission with you.

# Types of Commission

There are several different approaches to real estate agent commission, including a flat fee commission, a tiered commission, and a fixed-percentage commission. When you have a clear idea of how each method works, you can make an informed choice about which type of commission best fits you and your situation.

## Tiered Commission

A tiered commission is proportional to the final sale price of the property. It increases on a sliding scale so it can work as an added incentive for agents to achieve the best possible price. Tiered commissions can be negotiated in advance, before you sign an agreement with your agent.

## Flat Fee Commission

Some real estate agent commission is charged as a flat fee, regardless of how much the property sells for. This is an appealing option for many sellers because you know exactly what you will be paying. There is no standard real estate commission rate so this fee can also be negotiated.

## Fixed-Percentage

Many agents charge commission as a percentage of the final sale price. This should be agreed up front, along with an estimate for the value of your property, so you have a good idea of what to expect. This fee structure can be beneficial for both parties as the agent is motivated to get the best possible price.

# What Does an Agent's Commission Get You?

When you enlist the help of a real estate agent, you are partnering with the experts and benefitting from their experience, reputation and specialist skills. The right agent will bring invaluable insights into the local market, as well as giving you access to their contacts and databases of active buyers. They will be able to plan a strategic campaign for marketing and selling your property, using the most effective channels and techniques.

The amount that you pay in real estate agent commission will also get you expert advice about repairs, improvement and styling that could make all the difference to the sale of your home.

Your agent will be your point of contact with prospective buyers, coordinating and presenting each open house and actively working to sell the property to buyers in person. If you choose to sell your property at auction, your agent will also play a key role in conducting this. When it comes to negotiating with buyers, your agent will work on your behalf to secure the best price.
Real estate agent commission pays off in many different ways, including peace of mind and a stress-free experience, a quick and smooth sale, and a premium price.

# Selling Your Home with Calibre Real Estate

At Calibre, we offer industry experience and local market insights, with a personal and tailored approach. We are known for our transparency and integrity, and would be happy to discuss our real estate agent fees and structure in more detail so that you know where you stand.

Contact us today to find out what we could do for you.

# Real Estate Advertising Costs

Naturally, you want to keep the costs down when trying to sell your property, but real estate marketing costs and advertising fees are a necessary investment if you want maximum exposure and the best sale price. There is a sliding scale, but you will need to spend a certain amount in these areas if you want to see results.

Justin Hagen, Licensed Estate Agent at Calibre Real Estate, shares his professional opinion on how much you can expect to pay for quality real estate advertising and marketing.

## How Much Does Quality Real Estate Marketing Cost?

Below, you can find some typical costs for the different types of marketing output. Talk to a Calibre Real Estate agent to find out more about why each are important as well as some complimentary services.

### Professional Photography

Professional photography is one of the best ways of attracting buyers to your home. The price you pay for this service will depend on how many photographs you require, as well as the particular package you choose. Some photographers offer twilight or dusk shots to show your home in a particularly appealing light, the addition of virtual furniture, or drone footage to show off the plot as a whole.

approx. $200 – $500+

### A Detailed Floor Plan

Floor plans complement still photography by helping buyers to understand the proportions and aspect of each room, and how they connect together. A floor plan may be included as part of the photography package, or it could involve a small extra cost.

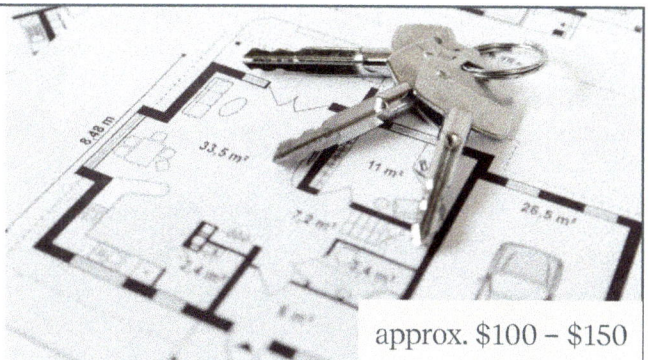

approx. $100 – $150

## Property Video

Video is a powerful asset as it has been shown to engage buyers on a deeper level than still photography. Moving images bring the rooms to life and helps buyers to imagine themselves in the property.

approx. $695

## Matterport Property Tour

3D virtual tours have proven to be invaluable in property marketing. They allow buyers to tour your home remotely and in their own time, giving you a much wider reach. An instant virtual tour is both highly efficient and effective in engaging prospective buyers with your property. To experience one of our recent Matterports for yourself, visit our website.

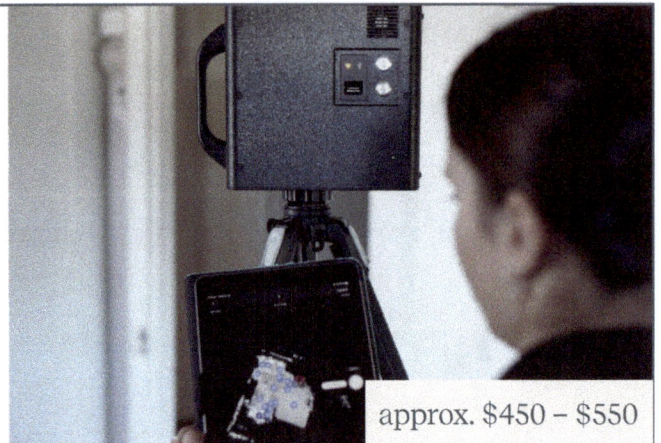

approx. $450 – $550

## Online Real Estate Sales Portals

Online sales portals are very often the first stop for people who are looking to buy. Sites such as domain.com.au and realestate.com.au compile huge numbers of property listings in a searchable format, making it quick and easy for buyers to find property matches in their area.

The cost to advertise on realestate.com.au, or a similar online portal, can vary dramatically as they offer various different packages. Your agent will be able to advise about the most relevant portals to use for your target market, and which package is right for you.

Agencies sometimes have their own sales portals where long time, engaged buyers looking in the area regularly check.

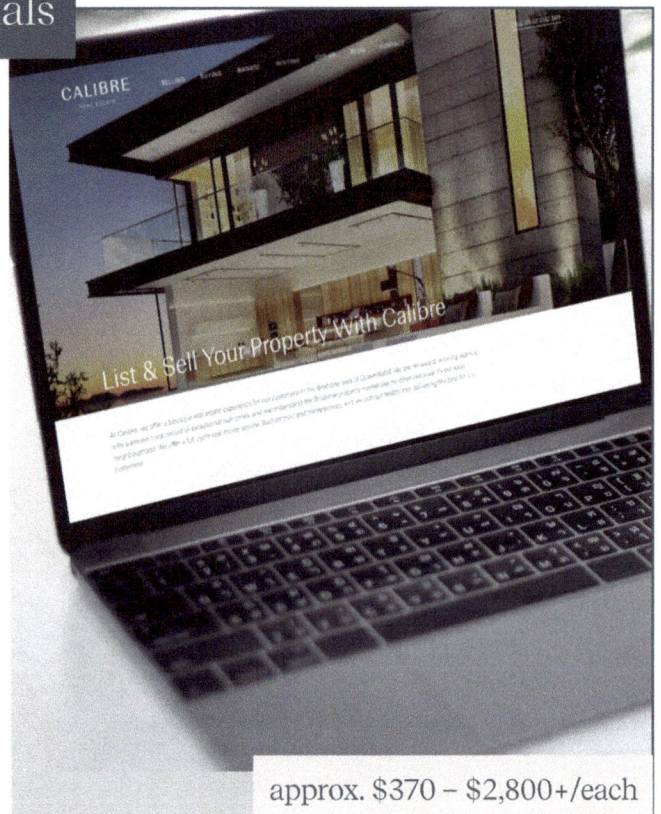

approx. $370 – $2,800+/each

## Professional Copywriting

Copywriting is about more than just listing the details of your property. Compelling copy can inspire buyers and get them excited about your property from the word go, so this can be a valuable asset in your marketing campaign. Some agencies will have in-house copywriters to write your listing, and produce copy for brochures and other marketing materials. Others will outsource to a copywriter and charge you an additional fee.

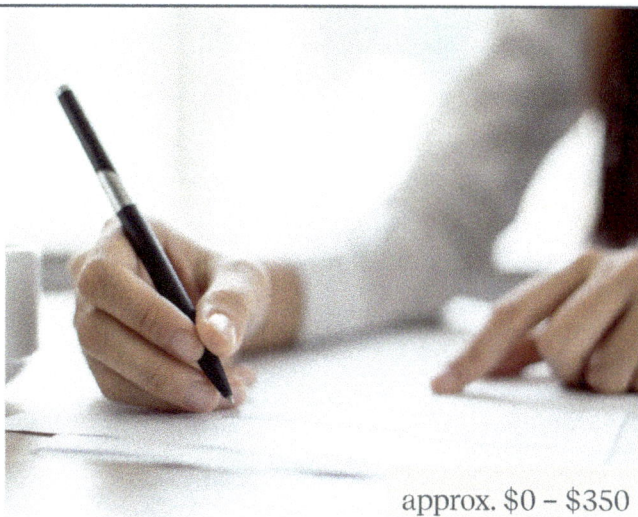

approx. $0 – $350

## Social Media Campaign

Targeted social media campaigns allow you to directly reach out to a wider audience of active buyers, and to motivate people who might be interested but who haven't yet taken the first step. Your agent will have experience of social media marketing so will be able to manage a strategic campaign for your property.

approx. $400

## Brochures

It is a good idea to have printed brochures on hand at every open house, so that prospective buyers can take one away with them.
A professionally designed brochure, printed on high quality paper or card, will cost more than an in-house brochure supplied by your agency. Your agent will be able to advise about how many copies to print so that you don't over-order and over-pay.

approx. $0 – $150+

## Property Signage

Signage options vary from the standard agency "For Sale" signboard to a sign that specifically showcases your property, with photos and tailored copywriting. It is important to check whether there are any local council restrictions on signage before putting one up outside your home, but they are an effective way to catch the eye of passers-by.

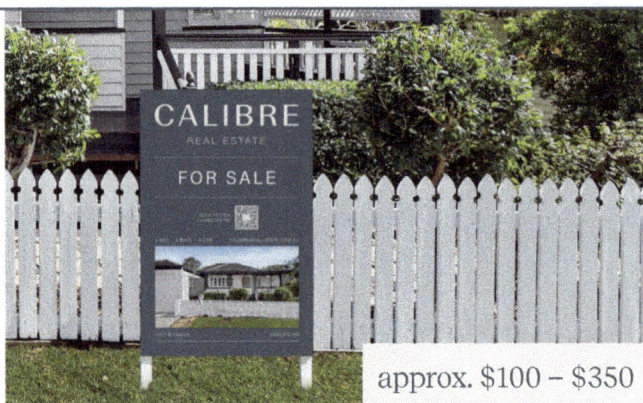

approx. $100 – $350

## Letterbox Dropping

Dropping printed cards through letterboxes in your local area is a simple and effective way of getting the word out about your property. The price will vary depending on the size, quantity and quality of the letterbox cards.

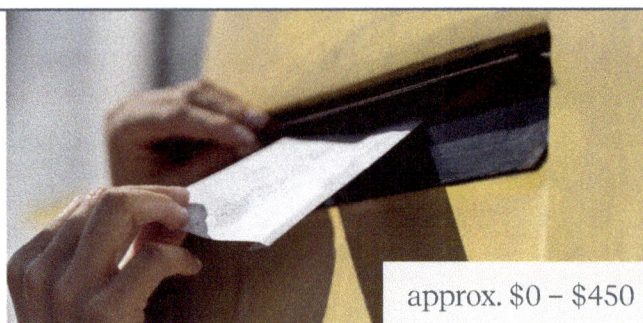

approx. $0 – $450

## Newspaper Advertising

A good number of prospective buyers still prefer to check property listings in print, so this is another avenue to consider. The cost of print advertisements will depend on the newspaper or publication, the size and location of the advert, and whether it includes images.

approx. $250+

## Additional Marketing

Additional marketing tools include things like SMS marketing, office window cards, open homes, and more... Your Calibre Real Estate agent will work with you to develop a strategic marketing campaign that combines various channels and media, while tailoring it to your goals and budget.

Calibre Real Estate's marketing campaigns find the balance between maximum exposure and engagement, and affordable property marketing costs that suit your budget. As we explore the various marketing options with you and offer expert and tailored advice, you can rest assured that we have done the very best to achieve the sale price your property deserves.

# Choosing an Agent

Your real estate agent will become your advisor, your support and your advocate throughout the process of selling your home, so it's crucial to do your research. It's important to know how to find a real estate agent you can trust, and what to look for when choosing a real estate agency. Here are some key areas to consider:

## Track Record

Experience is invaluable in this game. It pays to find a real estate agent who can demonstrate a track record of success with selling properties like yours – not just the number of completed sales, but also the sale prices they were able to achieve for their clients.

## Approach & Strategy

When choosing a real estate agency, ask about their proposed strategy for marketing and selling your home. A skilled and experienced agent will be able to immediately identify your target market, tailor their approach, and outline a multi-channel marketing strategy.

## Testimonials

When selecting an agent, you may wish to see some real qualitative feedback on their service. Testimonials are vital in the decision-making process.

## Communication

It's important that your agent listens to you, rather than just talking at you. They should be approachable, take the time to understand your individual circumstances and preferences, and also be able to clearly explain their advice and recommendations.

## Cost & Terms

Before choosing a real estate agency, make sure you understand their pricing structure, and what commission is involved, so that there are no hidden costs.

## Local Knowledge

Find a real estate agent with strong and up to date knowledge of the local neighbourhood and market trends!

Above all, look for experience and results! At Calibre, we are a fully licensed and award-winning real estate agency, with a proven track record of more than a decade of delivering exceptional outcomes for our customers. Guided by the core principles of integrity, transparency and trust, we put our customers first and pride ourselves on service. Talk to us today to find out what we can do for you – picking a real estate agent could be easier than you think!

# Why Sell With Calibre?

## 25%
We sell
properties
faster[1]

## 10+
Street records
broken by an agent
in 2021/2022 FY[2]

## 10/10
NPS score
(customer
satisfaction)[3]

## 20+
Real Estate
nominations
& awards[4]

## Exceptional Outcomes

At Calibre Real Estate, we deliver for our clients. We work on your behalf to secure the best sale price for your property, based on our local experience, marketing expertise, and negotiating skill. We have a strong reputation for quality, a track record of successful sales, and loyal customers who choose us again and again. Calibre is an award-winning agency with a complete suite of services to offer.

## Unrivalled Service

We are committed to giving our customers a positive experience, from beginning to end. With our personal service and transparent communication, we aim to take the stress, anxiety and uncertainty out of your real estate journey. Your dedicated Calibre agent is always on hand to answer your questions, offer advice, and work on your behalf to secure the best outcomes.

## Iconic Marketing

At Calibre Real Estate, we have a proven track record of marketing properties for success. We combine state-of-the-art tools and techniques with tried and tested traditional methods to showcase your property for maximum exposure. Our extensive experience, combined with in-depth insights and understanding of the local market, are what sets us apart.

SOURCE:
1– 2022 Q4 Sales data, office average 24 days, Brisbane average: 32 days
2– Justin Hagen's street records at time of sale for 2021/2022 FY
3– Customer Thermometer NPS scores in 2022 (Real estate sales)
4– 2010-2023

## Dream Team

The Calibre team is made up of experienced and dedicated professionals who are committed to delivering the best for our clients – in terms of service, experience and outcomes. We pride ourselves on being in touch with the local market, and with the latest tools and technologies, and we are always striving to learn more and stay ahead of the game.

## Solid Brand

Calibre Real Estate has a strong reputation as one of Queensland's most trusted names in local real estate. An award-winning brand, we are known for integrity, innovation and quality in every area of our work, and our track record speaks for itself. We have a loyal base of customers who recommend us to friends and family because of the unparalleled experience we offer our clients.

## Community Support Initiatives

We believe that real estate is not just about properties but about people and communities. At Calibre, we take seriously our responsibility to nurture growth and development by giving back to the communities in which we do business, and are proud to have led the way for others to follow.

## Testimonials

Our customers know they can trust us to put them first, with a personal service, clear communication, and excellent outcomes. Find out what they have to say about their experience with the team at Calibre.

# Where Next?

> The first step in selling your property is to get a realistic idea of how much you should ask for it. This will set you on track to targeting the right buyers and getting the best price, as well as helping you to plan ahead financially. There are various factors that can affect the valuation of your property, including location, type, size and condition of the property, and local demand from buyers. The best way to get a realistic and up to date valuation of your property is to speak to an agent who knows the market and has recent experience of selling similar properties in your area.

At Calibre Real Estate, we have extensive knowledge of your local area and a comprehensive understanding of the current market conditions. Our experienced agents know what buyers are looking for, and what they're willing to pay for a property like yours. We offer a free market appraisal, with no obligation, so you can get a detailed report for your property and know exactly where you stand.
Get in touch with our team today and we can help you take the first step towards a fast sale at the best price.

If you do choose to sell your home with Calibre Real Estate, we will create a customised sale strategy for you and your property, devised by local experts, that capitalises on every marketing channel and opportunity.

# Exceptional Outcomes

## Positive Experience

At Calibre Real Estate, we believe that selling your house or property can be a smooth, stress-free and exciting experience if you have the right team behind you. For more than a decade, we have been providing our customers with personal support and guidance so that you can enjoy peace of mind and a successful outcome.

## Unrivalled Service

As an established agency with a strong reputation, you can trust the skilled and experienced team at Calibre Real Estate to deliver a high quality, comprehensive service that puts you in control.

## Selling for the Best Price

We work tirelessly on your behalf to get the most out of your sale. From marketing and negotiating to the final settlement, our mission is to secure a premium price for your property so you don't have to settle for anything less.

## We Deliver More

We offer our customers the benefit of our extensive real estate experience, marketing expertise, and sales proficiency, and we do it all with your needs front and centre. Our reputation for outstanding service and our proven track record of impressive sales results speak for themselves – with Calibre Real Estate, you get more.

## Complete Suite of Services

From market analysis and property appraisals to marketing strategies and negotiating skill, the agents at Calibre Real Estate provide the complete package. Enjoy a premium and personal service from valuation to completion.

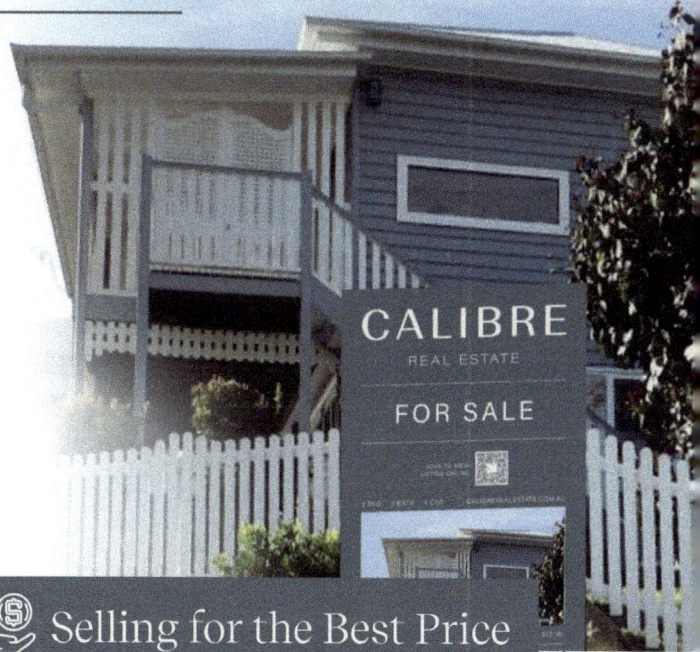

Selling your property is about more than just putting it on the market – that's when we get to work.

# Iconic Marketing

## Calibre's Iconic Marketing

At Calibre Real Estate, we know from experience that the way your home is marketed has a huge impact on its final sale price. We understand that simply displaying a 'For Sale' sign on the lawn and running an ad for an open house in the local paper is not going to cut it.

That's why we apply a strategic marketing methodology for maximum exposure. After all, the goal when marketing your home is to generate as much interest from buyers as possible, and that means getting it noticed by the right people.

We are experts at marketing properties for sales success. We know how to develop a tailored real estate marketing strategy that exploits and combines the wide-ranging tools and techniques available to showcase your property in the right ways, to the right people.

We use state-of-art solutions and digital marketing strategies, along with traditional in-person and print approaches, to give your property maximum exposure. We aim to run a promotion campaign blitz as soon as your home hits the market and we offer a number of comprehensive real estate marketing packages, which we tailor to meet your individual needs.

With access to some of the largest real estate databases in Australia, we are able to combine market analysis data with our own extensive experience in order to make strategic decisions in line with the latest market trends and developments.

Calibre Real Estate has been recognised with multiple awards since 2010, including the 2021 REIQ Multimedia Award. Quality is one of our hallmarks, so we are always working to monitor and improve the quality of our services so that we can continue to set the standard for our industry.

We believe that our customers deserve the very best, and that's why we market every home with creative energy, unrivalled skill, and meticulous attention to detail. It's the voices of our customers that matter most to us, so we conduct regular customer feedback surveys to make sure that we are delivering what we promise and scoring 'Excellent' across the board.

At Calibre Real Estate, we are always striving to improve and innovate without straying from our roots. We don't just focus on property; we focus on people. While so much happens online these days, we still thrive on the human touch as this is where real connection and relationships are forged. We believe in engaging with our buyers and sellers, and not just with electronic devices. Harnessing the power of modern digital marketing solutions, in line with our values, we are able to stay at the cutting edge of real estate marketing and promotion without compromising on our commitment to people.

Here we look at the most tried and tested strategies of marketing in real estate, plus newer marketing strategies and techniques that have the potential to propel your listing beyond the competition.

## The Importance of a Powerful Marketing Plan

The key to success in real estate marketing is planning and preparation. Your agent should be able to outline a clear and focused marketing strategy, based on proven methods and a track record of successful sales. At Calibre Real Estate, we will work with you to develop a plan that is appropriate to your property type and area, and to your needs and preferences.

With our industry experience and local market insights, we can advise you about the most effective ways to gain maximum exposure and attract the most interested buyers.

The best marketing strategies combine digital, SEO and social media promotion with things like real estate marketing flyers and brochures, prints ads, signboards, and good old letter box drops. More exposure means more interest from buyers, and more competition means a higher sale price.

## Real Estate Portals – Rich Online Presence

It's no secret that the vast majority of buyers – over 85% – use online property searches to kick off their house hunt, and it's often property portals such as realestate.com.au that are the first port of call. If you want to get your property noticed fast, by as many prospective buyers as possible, your marketing campaign must include these channels. These property search websites are hotbeds for people who are actively looking to buy, so the potential for converting interest into offers is high.

With Calibre Real Estate, you have the opportunity to list your property on over a dozen of the most popular real estate websites, including our own premium, mobile-friendly portal. We will also run comprehensive real estate social media marketing campaigns to promote your property through our social channels and

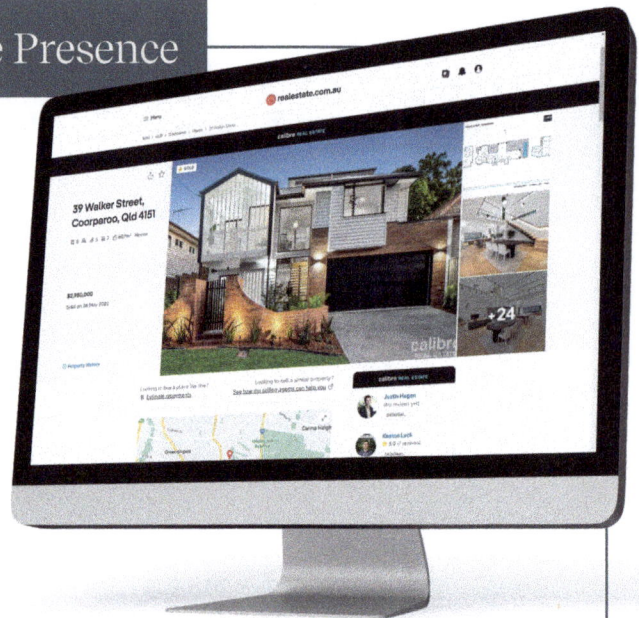

get it seen by an even wider audience. We encourage buyers to set property alerts so that they get notified of any new properties listed with Calibre Real Estate that meet their criteria. This means the right buyers are instantly alerted to your property and directed to your listing. These are just some of the ways in which we work on behalf of our customers to achieve a fast and lucrative sale.

## Large Scale Email Marketing

As a respected property marketing agency with a solid reputation, we have a database of thousands of potential buyers in each of our areas of operation. When you list your property with us, we will instantly let the relevant buyers know about it, and use targeted e-mail campaigns to generate interest from active buyers in your local area.

## Advanced Search Engine Marketing

We have expertise in running successful Google ad campaigns to attract active buyers and sellers and promote properties effectively. Our real estate SEO marketing campaigns are strategic and targeted so that we can match relevant properties with people who are actively looking to buy. This means more completed sales, with positive outcomes for our customers.

## Outstanding Social Media Marketing

Social media is an ever more powerful tool in the industry, from real estate Facebook marketing to paid campaigns and advertising across every platform. At Calibre Real Estate, we have joined forced with Properti to create an automated Facebook and Instagram advertising platform for our customers, which intensifies the promotion of our property listings and drives maximum exposure and engagement. This state-of-the-art platform also enables us to analyse behaviour, trends and responses to our posts so that we can be sure to put the right properties in front of the right audience when it counts.

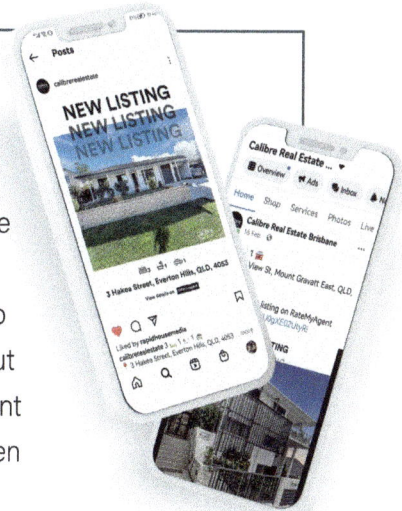

# Effective Video Marketing

We understand the power of video to catch the attention of prospective buyers. Our strategic video marketing starts with a presentation and tour of the property, which we share on social media, as well as ongoing video marketing campaigns through platforms such as Google and Facebook.

## What makes video marketing such a valuable resource for your property sale?

- ☑ The power of the moving image offers potential buyers a unique feel of the home, and conveys more than static photos
- ☑ Video can be used effectively through email marketing and social media
- ☑ Interest generated via video leads to more clicks on your property listing
- ☑ These clicks translate into more people at your open house
- ☑ More inspections means more offers
- ☑ The more offers on the table, the better price your real estate agent can secure!

At Calibre Real Estate, we have the experience and skill to use this powerful tool to its full potential and achieve the best results for you.

# Professional Photography, Videography and 3D Property Tours

We understand the importance of capturing a buyer's attention in an instant. That's why we work with exceptional photographers and videographers to produce high quality media that showcases your property at its very best. First impressions count, and we go the extra mile to stop any interested buyer in their tracks.

## Professional Photos

With so many people searching for properties online these days, high quality professional photography really is a non-negotiable. It doesn't take much for a buyer to move on to the next listing, so you really have to make yours stand out.

At Calibre Real Estate, our photography is presented to the highest standard, and with exceptional attention to detail, highlighting the best features of your home.

### Only the Best Shots

A professional real estate photographer is responsible for capturing only the best shots of your home. They will dictate how to manipulate the space, where to create horizontal and vertical lines, and how to direct the focus. From selecting the most picture-worthy areas, to capturing shots at the right time of day, the photographer will curate a story for your potential buyers to explore.

### Post-Production

During the post-production phase, the finest photos will be chosen and tastefully enhanced to present your property in the best light. With professional photos capturing your property in all its glory, buyers are much more likely to take notice. This generates more inspections and, ultimately, more offers. Real estate photography is not a liability expense – when done right, it can only serve to be beneficial for your home sale and almost always delivers a solid return on investment.

### Property Videos

Stunning photography is one thing, but a great property video can work wonders when it comes to selling your home. Gone are the days when professional property videos were only used at the highest end of luxury real estate marketing. At Calibre, we combine the benefits of professional photography and video marketing strategies, as well as cutting edge drone footage, to create a unique and enticing marketing campaign for your property that is sure to secure a premium price.

Presented by Calibre Real Estate Brisbane, AU
404/50 Sylvan Road, Toowong

# 3D Property Tours

The Matterport 3D property tour enables users to move through a property and see it from any angle, almost as if viewing it in person. Since REA Group began using Matterport on its partner site, realestate.com.au, it found a significant increase in the engagement levels of potential buyers. According to REA, buyers are 60% more likely to email and 95% more likely to call an agent about a property that includes a 3D property tour. That's a pretty big swing!

High quality 3D property tours make it even easier for more buyers to view and explore your home in their own time. The tour is available 24/7, so they don't have to wait for an in-person inspection before falling in love with your property. A virtual tour also gives you greater reach, as interstate buyers are able to discover your property remotely.

When relocating from overseas, Calibre tenant Lawson and his family were finding it difficult to secure a new property to lease before their move. Thanks to Matterport 3D technology, Lawson was able to experience a realistic property visit, moving from room to room and exploring the property in detail, while still being fully remote. This is what made the difference for them. "We found the 3D property tour to be indispensable," explains Lawson. "It was just like taking a walk-through of the house. Best of all, we didn't have to fly there to do it in person. Initially we were considering just waiting until we arrived. Thankfully, the 3D property tour helped us to have the confidence to go ahead. Now we have a place waiting for us when we arrive."

01

02

### We do more to turn heads.

Great real estate marketing is all about getting as many eyes as possible on your listing, and grabbing the attention of active buyers. At Calibre Real Estate, we go above and beyond to turn heads in your direction.

## Creative Professional Copywriting

Selling a property is about more than facts, stats and feature checklists. As well as giving potential buyers the headlines about your property, we use narrative storytelling to help them fall in love with more than just the four walls. Through creative and well-crafted copy, we paint a compelling picture that invites buyers to envision the experience of living and enjoying their lives in this new home. We work with outstanding professional copywriters to connect with buyers on an emotional and aspirational level – if we can move the heart, we can move the head.

# Eye-Catching Signboards and Brochures

There's a reason why physical signboards on the street are still a staple of marketing in real estate. They are an economical, easy and effective way of capturing the attention of local people who may then become prospective buyers. A signboard is like waving a flag for your property, letting people know that it's available, and giving a quick snapshot of the key selling features to passers-by.

We also produce high quality property brochures and letter box cards that showcase your home in beautiful detail via stunning photographs and descriptive copy. These can be handed out at inspection visits, displayed in our local office window, and dropped through letter boxes to put your home on the radar with the locals.
We always include our estate agent contact details so that interested buyers can get in touch with us at Calibre to find out more and arrange a visit.

## Unique Pre-Market Preparation & Styling

Professional property styling has been proven to increase interest from potential buyers, reduce time on the market, and boost final sales prices by 10% on average. It can come down to just a few small changes and it's well worth the effort. Home styling includes general cleaning, decluttering and de-personalising so that the rooms feel fresh and spacious, and buyers can mentally move themselves in. You may also want to think about rearranging some of the existing furniture, accessories and lighting to show each room at its best, and even hiring a few items to refurnish or redecorate the space. Home styling is about selling an aspirational vision of what your property could be.

At Calibre Real Estate, we work with expert stylists at TheStyledHouse to help our clients with styling and staging. These friendly professionals are on hand to highlight the small things you can do to make a difference to your sale.

To find out what you can do to enhance each area of your home and get the most out of buyer inspections, download our Styling to Sell eBook.

## Calibre & Community Brand Magazine

Calibre & Community is our print and digital magazine. This is another powerful avenue for reaching buyers with our property listings, but it's also a way for us to build and nurture community around our area of passion and expertise. As well as articles about real estate, we feature style, food, fashion and philanthropy.

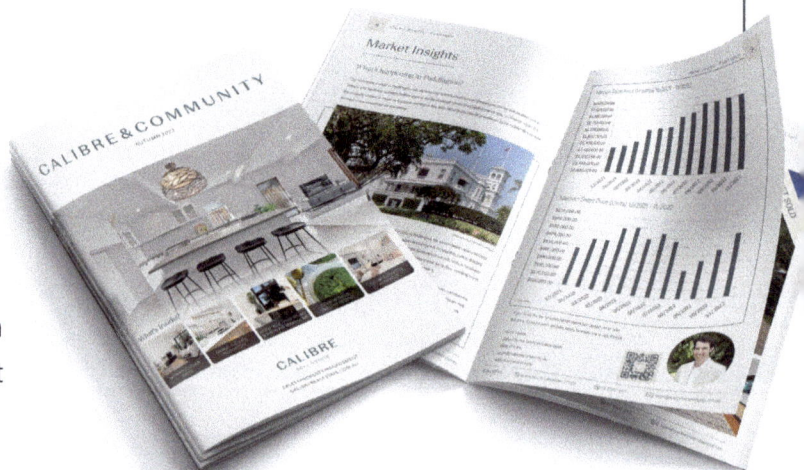

# Sell your home your way, with a tailored solution from the experts.

When it comes to selling your property in Brisbane, you really don't need to look any further. Here at Calibre Real Estate, we have the industry experience, the well-honed marketing tools and techniques, and the proven track record to deliver exceptional outcomes.  On top of that, we take a personalised approach that's tailored to your needs, circumstances and preferences.

Our expert knowledge of the areas we cover, paired with our commitment to our clients, makes us the only partner you need for a fast and successful sale. Contact your local Calibre Real Estate expert to discuss your customised marketing campaign and start your journey today.

List Your Home with Calibre Real Estate – Request a free property appraisal now!

# Unrivalled Service

Successful outcomes are one thing, but we understand that the experience of selling a property can live long in the memory – whether positive or negative. At Calibre Real Estate, we are committed to putting our customers first, and providing the highest quality of service from start to finish. We do this through personal and dedicated support, honest and transparent communication, and delivering on our promises.

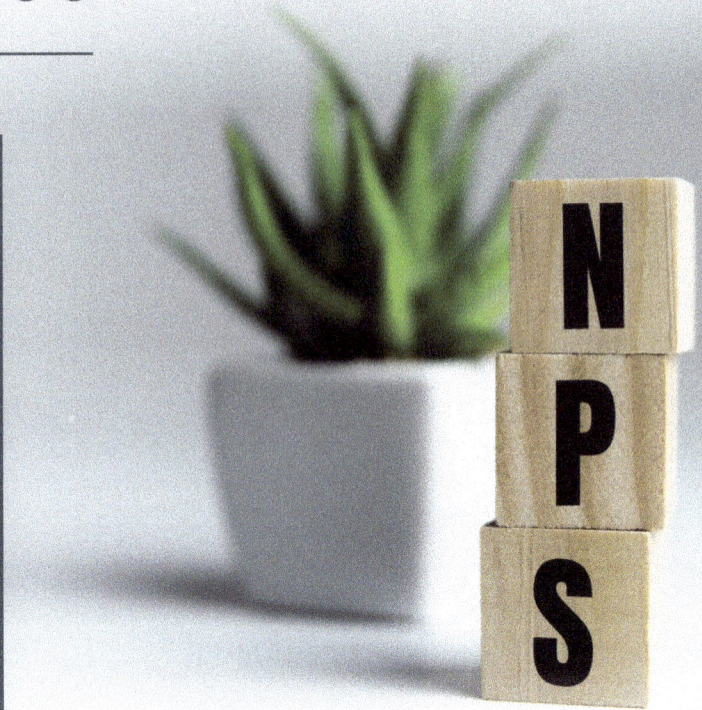

Over recent years, we have surveyed previous clients to let us know what we're doing right and where we can do better. We are committed to an ongoing process of learning and improving our offering for the benefit of our customers.

We are pleased to say that our overall NPS satisfaction score is currently 10/10*.
We remain committed to performing at this level and giving every customer the 10/10 experience as we cement a reputation as the 'Customer Experience Brand' in real estate.

*source: Customer Thermometer NPS scores by vendors in 2022

## Transparent Communication

In our experience, one of the key ways to give customers a positive and stress-free experience of selling their property is through regular and transparent communication. We specialise in providing expert advice and support with decision-making, answering your questions and clearing up confusion, and delivering a detailed plan that lets you know exactly what's going to happen, when, and why. Our goal is to remove the stress, anxiety and uncertainty so that you can understand and even enjoy the process.

## Personal Support

No two properties and no two clients are the same. We have no one-size-fits-all model for marketing and selling your home. Your Calibre Real Estate agent will take the time to understand your specific circumstances, your reasons and motivations for selling, your priorities and your preferences. It may be that you need to sell fast, or that you want to wait for the most favourable market conditions so that you can secure the very best price. Your dedicated agent will work with you to develop a comprehensive and customised marketing plan that suits you.

## Delivering Results

We take pride in delivering on our promises, and our exceptional outcomes speak for themselves. We aim to get your property sold quickly, easily, and at the best price. Guided by you and your objectives for the sale, your agent will work on your behalf, from marketing to negotiations and settlement. Thanks to our local knowledge and experience, our comprehensive marketing expertise, and our proven track record, we are confident that we can deliver for you.

Your Journey Starts Here – List with the best.

CALIBRE REAL ESTATE  ⊕ www.calibrerealestate.com.au  📞 07 3367 3411  ✉ yourwayhome@calibrerealestate.com.au

# Dream Team

It is our mission to give every customer an unforgettable experience, with a highly personal touch. We are a team of talented and experienced real estate professionals, dedicated to serving our customers and maintaining the highest quality standards. Through regular training, in-touch market awareness and insights, and the latest in marketing techniques and technologies, we strive to set ourselves apart from the competition and deliver more for our clients.

The Calibre Real Estate reputation is grounded in values of integrity, trust, and determination on behalf of our clients. Our people love what they do, and we believe that our customers and communities deserve the best from us.

All Calibre Real Estate agents are fully qualified in accordance with local legislation, and this is combined with the high standards that we set for ourselves.

# Solid Brand

Established in 2009 by Alice and Justin Hagen, Calibre Real Estate is now widely recognised as one of Queensland's most trusted local real estate brands.

Our success is founded on innovation, reliability, and a commitment to our customers. The Calibre team is a community of dedicated professionals who are motivated to deliver the very best for every client.

We have been repeatedly recognised as industry leaders, with an Award for Growth and Innovation, Awards for Excellence – Community Service, Top 100 Fastest Growing, Awards for Excellence – Large Agency of the Year, Young Entrepreneur Awards – Property & Construction, Multimedia Awards, and many others.

When it came to buying their own home, over a decade ago, Alice and Justin Hagen struggled to find an agent who would take the time to listen to their particular needs and circumstances. They wanted a real estate agency that could offer a professional and sophisticated service but with a personal, boutique approach. They were looking for an agent who was fully on their side, who they could trust to work on their behalf to achieve their goals, and this just didn't seem to be the norm. When they founded the company in 2009, their vision was to reinvent real estate, and this is what continues to drive Calibre's success today.

By listening to you, and understanding your priorities and motivations, we can provide a completely tailored approach that fits your needs. We combine this with over a decade of industry experience, superior local knowledge, specialist marketing expertise and industry-leading techniques to deliver a comprehensive service that is both meticulously professional and highly personal.

# Calibre's Community Support Initiatives

We believe that real estate is about more than just buying and selling properties. We see our role as a vital contributor to the building of neighbourhoods and suburbs, and bringing people and communities together.

We nurture community growth and development by giving back to the communities we serve, and we were the first in our industry to do this. While a handful of others have since followed in our footsteps, we are proud to have led the way.

## Recent community initiatives include:

- The Good Box (helping Australians who are experiencing homelessness)
- Mater Dei P&F
- R U OK? Day
- Cancer Council
- Brain Child

- The Legacy Organisation (Supporting the families of our veterans)
- Ashgrove State School P&C
- Women's Legal Services
- Royal Brisbane and Women's Hospital Foundation

# Calibre & Community Brand Magazine

Calibre & Community, our print and digital magazine, features articles about real estate, style, food, fashion and philanthropy. There is also a section devoted entirely to supporting and celebrating local businesses, such as cafes, restaurants, shops, and cinemas.

In every edition, we shine a spotlight on two or three new businesses, and we also offer free opportunities for other businesses to promote new products, services or special offers, share their upcoming events, or simply reach new audiences.

The magazine has thousands of online readers every month, in Queensland and across Australia, while printed copies of Calibre & Community are available from many locations around Brisbane.

# Testimonials

Our customers know they can trust us to put them first, with a personal service, clear communication, and excellent outcomes. These are the voices that matter most to us, and this is why we take great pride in what we do. We love to hear from our customers because we are always open to learning about what we're getting right and what we can do better. Find out what they have to say about their experience with the team at Calibre.

**Errol Cooke / Google reviews**

★ ★ ★ ★ ★

What an amazing team they have at Calibre – reliable, professional, diligent and personable. I have dealt with many agents over the years but Calibre has been, without a doubt, the best I've worked with. I would highly recommend this agency.

**Chloe Zhao / Google reviews**

★ ★ ★ ★ ★

It makes a difference to have a real estate agency with an owner that  actually cares about customer service, and really goes out of their way to help. I just wanted to say thanks to Calibre Real Estate and the team for always being there!

**Matt Beauchamp / Google reviews**

★ ★ ★ ★ ★

I can highly recommend Calibre's services for both sales and property management. They are always more than happy to help, providing great advice and strategies.

**Kathryn Jones / Google reviews**

★ ★ ★ ★ ★

A friendly, approachable and professional team! I wouldn't hesitate to recommend their services.

**Susan Laws / Google reviews**

★ ★ ★ ★ ★

The team at Calibre made the sale of my house a very easy process. They were always positive and a pleasure to deal with. I'm very happy with the outcome of the sale. I highly recommend Calibre Real Estate!

CALIBRE
REAL ESTATE

**Leslee Mackay / Google reviews**

★ ★ ★ ★ ★

The Calibre Real Estate team sold my home in Moggill. I cannot thank them enough for their hard work and dedication. They were always extremely professional, punctual and honest.

After listing with another agent for over 6 months with no result, I now realise that if I had chosen Calibre Real Estate from the start I could have saved myself a lot of time, effort and money.

**Rachel Hawyes / Google reviews**

★ ★ ★ ★ ★

Calibre managed our investment property for 4 years without issue, and then sold it for us in record time for a great price. Highly recommended.

**Adrian Stagg / Google reviews**

★ ★ ★ ★ ★

I found Calibre Real Estate to be good, honest people to deal with. You can trust them.

**Jaga & Jan / RateMyAgent reviews**

★ ★ ★ ★ ★

Besides being highly accomplished and professional real estate agents, the Calibre team are also the nicest and most sincere people you could hope to meet. They helped us with both the purchase of our new property and the sale of our existing property. The entire process was handled with the utmost care and attention to detail and we are happy to recommend Calibre to anyone looking to buy or sell property.

**Kay Chris / RateMyAgent reviews**

★ ★ ★ ★ ★

A great team to work with! The property had previously been on the market with another agent for 90 days. We took the Calibre team's advice and undertook some minor repairs, which significantly added to buyer attraction and achieved the result we wanted. They also suggested that we have the power on to show the house in its best light – particularly for evening viewings. I cannot understand why we were not advised this previously!

**Linda / RateMyAgent reviews**

★ ★ ★ ★ ★

I cannot speak highly enough of the Calibre team. They showed a really good understanding of the market, and how to get a quick sale at the best price. The Calibre agents had fantastic and innovative strategies to generate interest in my property, and this really helped to ensure a consistently high number of viewings until I received the offer I'd been waiting for! They then put in 110% to make sure that the sale went through successfully, including advising on my move to my new property – truly fantastic service! My property looked stunning and I could see that my house sold before others that were listed at the same time. This, I am sure, was down to the presentation and marketing provided by the Calibre team. I highly recommend Calibre!

# About Calibre Real Estate

## About Calibre

Calibre is an award-winning boutique real estate agency serving the Brisbane area with full cycle real estate services. We are a local team of fully qualified and dedicated real estate agents who specialise in supporting our clients throughout their property journey. We are known for our outstanding customer service, transparent communication, and exceptional outcomes.

## Our History/Heritage

Established more than a decade ago, Calibre is a family business with family values and these principles of integrity and trust continue to provide the foundation for our personal customer service. We work in partnership with our customers and develop lasting relationships. We were born and raised in Brisbane, and we love to serve our local community with quality real estate services.

## Our Team

Our agents are the best of the best. We live locally, and we know the Brisbane property market like no other. Our dream team is built around a shared commitment to excellence and a personal dedication to our loyal customers. We are all fully qualified and experienced agents, and we love what we do.

## Our Values

The values that shape and define Calibre are trust, integrity and quality. We are known for our open, honest and transparent communication and our unrivalled customer service.

## Why Choose Calibre

We are here to support you in your real estate journey, from beginning to end, giving you the benefit of our experience and proven strategies. Our team is local to the Brisbane area, so we have an intimate and invaluable understanding of the local property market and current trends, which equips us to get the best outcomes for you. We have a solid track record and our achievements have been recognised with multiple industry awards. When you choose Calibre, you choose a real estate partner you can depend on.

## Supporting Our Community

At Calibre, we understand that real estate is about more than property transactions. We believe that we have a vital role to play in building neighbourhoods and bringing communities together, and we take this responsibility seriously. We have led the way in investing in community growth and development, and giving back to the communities we serve, through initiatives such as Cancer Council, The Legacy Organisation, and Brain Child.

## Experience the Calibre Difference

As a boutique agency, with a local team, we are able to provide a dedicated and personal level of service that you wouldn't get with many larger agencies. We put our customers first and show exceptional attention to detail. When you partner with a Calibre real estate agent you get an experienced and knowledgeable advisor, and a trusted advocate.

# What's My House Worth?
# Free Property Appraisal

## Time to sell? What's My House Worth?

Put simply, your property is worth what someone is willing to pay for it in the current market.
To get an accurate property value estimate, request an in-person or online home appraisal from
a Calibre Real Estate expert.

It's free, fast, and there's absolutely no obligation.

## Ready to get in the know?

An appraisal is a detailed property value check that takes into account the type, size and location of your
home, and looks at how it compares to other similar properties in the local area. It can also include
recommendations for improvements to help you get more from your sale.

To get clued up about where your house stands in the market today, visit our website, fill in your details
and we'll get right back to you to arrange your free property value estimate.

# What does a property appraisal include?

## A Comprehensive Assessment

One of our agents will review your property, looking at its size, number of bedrooms and bathrooms, its general condition, fixtures and fittings, and the quality of any works or extensions. They will note particular selling features, as well as recommending any upgrades or improvements to your house that may be beneficial when the time comes to sell.

### Size

A complete assessment of your home, from bedrooms and bathrooms to living areas and outside space.

### Market Conditions

A detailed market analysis that takes into account current trends and recent sales of similar properties in the area.

### Location

An assessment of your property's general location – the desirability of the local area, and proximity to shops, schools and other amenities. This can also include your property's specific street location and curb appeal.

### Property Price Guide

We can provide you with a price guide or house value estimate at any time, to give you a realistic idea of your starting point from local real estate experts.

### Local Buyer Perspectives

Your local Calibre Real Estate agents have an in-depth knowledge of what buyers in your local area are looking for, and what makes a property more desirable to them. During your appraisal visit, they can pass on these insights and give you some recommendations for maximizing the value of your home in the eyes of potential buyers.

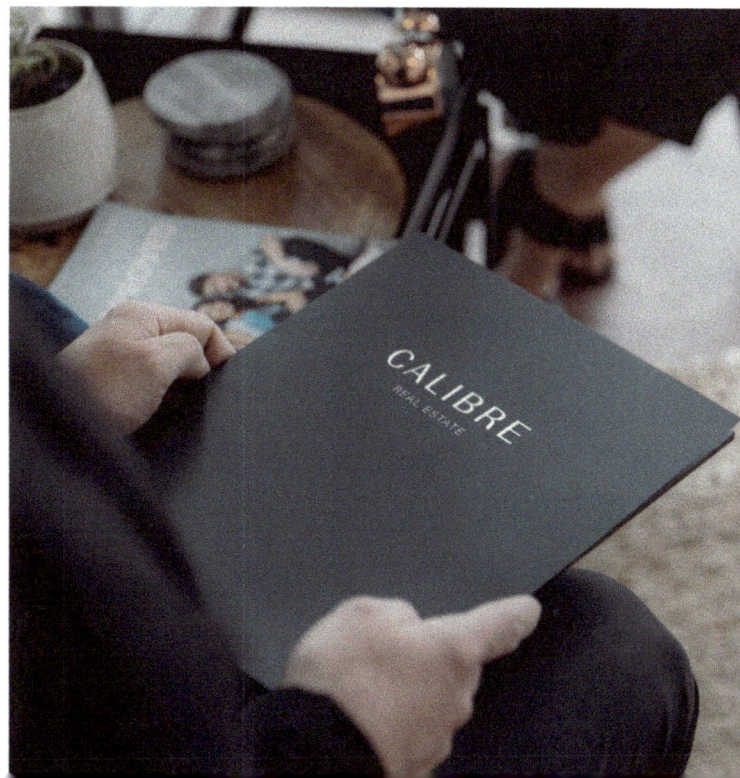

# Get your free appraisal in 3 simple steps

Connect with one of our local agents in person or via video call, and get your house valuation in just a few easy steps.

## 1

### Book your appraisal.

Complete the form with your contact details and your preference for an in person or virtual visit.

## 2

### Property visit.

Your local Calibre agent will be in touch to organise an informal visit at a date and time that works for you.

## 3

### Appraisal report.

You will receive a comprehensive property valuation report, an overview of the current market, and an accurate price guide.

Book your appraisal

# It pays to be in the know with a property price guide

Having an accurate idea of your real estate property value is useful at any time – not just when you're thinking of selling up. A free house valuation gives you a clearer picture of your own net worth and financial position, and helps you to make smart and informed decisions.

## THERE ARE PLENTY OF SCENARIOS WHERE A PROPERTY VALUATION MAKES GOOD SENSE:

- If you want to gain a better understanding of market fluctuations in your local area, and what they mean for the value of your property.

- When considering an extension or renovation and you want to stay in line with what buyers are looking for from houses in your area.

- To avoid pricing your property out of the market with costly renovations.

- When you want to find out the impact of your home improvement works on the market value of your property.

- If you're looking to re-mortgage or withdraw some capital from the equity of your property and want to know how much it's currently worth.

# Let's Get Moving

Hopefully you feel a bit more clued up about the process of selling your home, and the key points to bear in mind for getting the most out of your sale. We know there's a lot to take in, but this is this is what we do. We're here to support our clients from day one, and deliver the best results possible.

Request a free property appraisal now, and let's get to work!

# Property Management

A rental property can be a lucrative investment, but it's also a full-time job. In order to minimise the risk and maximise the returns you have to be proactive, organised, and in the know. That's where the services of an experienced local property management agency can be invaluable. At Calibre, our property management team provides our clients with comprehensive, hands-on, and tailored services so that you can enjoy the benefits of a successful rental property without the headaches.

## OUR PROPERTY MANAGEMENT SERVICES INCLUDE...

- Marketing and advertising
- Timely and transparent communication between parties
- Maintenance – Inspections, reports, and enlisting licensed tradespeople to act promptly
- Securing and retaining reliable tenants
- Preparation of policies and documentation
- Management of all property accounts – insurance, council, utilities, repairs and maintenance

## You stay in control...

- ☑ Final decision on tenants
- ☑ Timely payments and comprehensive financial records
- ☑ Detailed reports of the condition of the property

The experts at Calibre are always up to date with the latest market trends, demand, competition, and legislation. We have strict policies and proven procedures to protect you from risk and loss. Our priority is to maximise the potential of your rental investment, while giving you the peace of mind that your property is in the best hands.

Contact us today for your free rental appraisal or consultation.

Book your rental appraisal